Songs from the Eleventh Month

Elizabeth Clayton

Trafford
PUBLISHING™

Order this book online at www.trafford.com/08-0999
or email orders@trafford.com

Most Trafford titles are also available at major online book retailers.

Cover Design/Artwork: Elizabeth Clayton and Lynn O. Waltman
Designed by: Elizabeth Clayton
Photography: Lynn O. Waltman
Editor: Lynn O. Waltman

Note for Librarians: A cataloguing record for this book is available from Library and Archives Canada at www.collectionscanada.ca/amicus/index-e.html

ISBN: 978-1-4251-8479-7

Trafford PUBLISHING www.trafford.com

North America & international
toll-free: 1 888 232 4444 (USA & Canada)
phone: 250 383 6864 • fax: 250 383 6804 • email: info@trafford.com

The United Kingdom & Europe
phone: +44 (0)1865 487 395 • local rate: 0845 230 9601
facsimile: +44 (0)1865 481 507 • email: info.uk@trafford.com

10 9 8 7 6 5 4 3 2 1

Hickory in Autumn, One

Every leaf of the tree I came to see today
Was brilliant gold,
To fall before I see it again;
But in the moments of my viewing,
All that I could see,
Think, feel was that every leaf
Was brilliant in its
Moment of gold.

Elizabeth

Early November, 2005

Preface

The verses which comprise this small volume were written quite without ceremony or any thought that they would be read by many others. They are the unplanned but comfortable musings of an individual as a month in the changing seasons, summer to autumn, came and passed into yesterday. I am thoughtful in all seasons for nature is very close to me; it reflects the brilliantly gentle beauty of life and the sometime cruel and violent realities of existence, offering subjects for thoughts – questioning, struggle and thanksgiving.

The verses are of assorted themes, with prayers, and follow no pattern; the style is that of all my verse, free verse, for I do not feel content with rules in recording spontaneous thought and feeling. Since poetry is spontaneous, it should be so recorded. The illustrations are as the verses, outreachings of my thought in color and form rather than in words. They were drawn to the side of the verse as I wrote and later cut and painted with acrylics and oil, to be placed with their verses.

The entire volume is a piece of free association, out myself, in word, color, and form. The thoughts recorded, and embellished, are simply an extended expression of my whole being, suggested by friends to be published for others to enjoy.

Elizabeth

April 3, 2008

"Study nature as the countenance of God",
Charles Kingsly – "the sky, the seas,
the very landscape of thought."

Elizabeth

Table of Contents

songs
from the eleventh
month
elizabeth
october 31- november 31,
2003

— so little

— so little needed, to go to bed on:
the chartreuse oak,
small ballerina
leaning into her right toe;
my new rose, furry
crab, a deep blush hiding,
but escaping in secret smile;
and looking up, a pentangle
of blackbirds,
shadowed behind of the rising
light in the last October
quarter moon—
these, in the dying twilight, to, in
my beggar soul, know
beautiful repose:
I hold you, these, thee of the voiced good, to
and you bless me, to go to
bed on.

October 31, 2003 elizabeth

I feel a Presence about me,
but I feel that, also,
in the course of the day,
I must do my part;
and so,
the riddle establishes;
one which has beadings
and patterns
I cannot anticipate:
where do I begin and conclude—
perhaps always within
Presence; peace—
elizabeth

november 3, 2003
Borg's book completed,
learning center experience
finished.

thoughts,
one
because rain is forecast, the
hickory's gold will fly today,
lost magnificence,
into Presence, keeper of all seasons,
and as early morning sunlight,
in pale, lighted ivory, begs
acknowledgement,
I feel alone, the leaf drifting
downward
from trees now lost of their
dress, lines
of spilling black ink, small
into the sky, larger where
it falls to the constant
earth —
these with me, in the coming closing,
but bound in care of Presence.

sentiment fills the every
room of my heart, and
I recognize pain,
in looking behind,

in adulterated trepidation
before,
but most, O Presence, close
softly about me,
for I love.
into Thee, out of Thee, my
path as veiled as the
day lost to twilight, the thinker
to his postulates,
feather and wool me so that
I will be, of Thee,
safe and warm, become, again,
the broken dragon's wing,
within revelation's fire,
inside my childhood eye.

november 3, 2003 elizabeth

thoughts,
two
a handsome brocade, of distant
wheels, their echoes forming
raindrops around
reluctantly falling leaves;
pale morning's light
drawing memory over me,
like a sweet coverlet;
time and time, into season when
small, yellow butterflies
have flown into the
summers sun:
Please, please, Rational Construct
or mystic touch, hold me
in constancy
of well-thinking, in the
joy of thanksgivings;

background and surface,
highlights and shadow,
arrange me,
a pattern beautiful,
of a gentle peace.

Elizabeth

thoughts from my bedroom
November 5, 2003
7 - 8:30 AM

thoughts,
three

I kneel and spread my hands,
I spread all my heart,
open fans
whose faces beg of Thee,
O Holy Father God:
let the foxes which steal
my separate moments,
my sweet grapes,
let them be vanquished by
Thy light into my soul
a hunter's moon to find
and put to rout
all takers of good.
autumn insects sing through the
open door, in early evening
hours,

and the day reviewed,
stepping quickly into
yesterday, and fencing
thoughts of tomorrow.

O Holy Father God,
Presence, Thou to Cover, and
balm, to hold up and let
my heart to sing, Come,
I beg Thee, Come—
light to strike, balm
to soothe,
peace before quiet, in an
evening's silent hymn.

Amen.

Unhappy Thoughts
8:15 pm.
November 5, 2003

Elizabeth

november images

days journey by, slowly, quietly,
and upon reflection,
recognizably,
quickly; so that they arrange
one, onto the other, empty
spaces,
hollow soundings, the
grey of november.

as ice or candle settles into
the pool of its own self,
quite without
distinguishable form,
it stands
nonetheless, a reality,
metamorphosed,
a passing;

these toward yesterday,
and,
often gracious, but often,
unwanted forgetfulness,

elizabeth

november 8, 2003

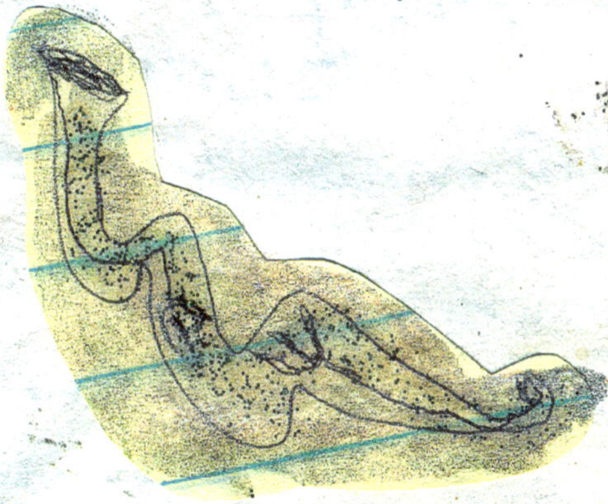

I am, Joseph, truly grandiose
in long moments, when
the widening expanses,
the intense of color, the
deepest timbres catch
my heart;
but I also dwell in the
thoughtful small, the
diminutive
becoming beautiful.
And so,
I watch you through your voice,
in your larger struggle,
but, too,
in the roll call of smaller
pathos;

And I love you in a kind
of desperation,
wishing that I could gather
the birth of your soul
into arms of just
a small comforting
safety,
And that over and again,
Elizabeth

Saturday,
November 8, 2003

the whisper

pouring from its intensely visable
circle,
streams out the halo, pure
white gold,
burnt, completely purged
mystic ash, that which
could lift as beloved saints,
into its own pouring down;
the spectacle spread over my
thought,
and it feigned, for a long
moment,
all poverty, all loss, israel
ever was,
with the passing of this splendor,
again, after captivity and
slave,
pilgrim and wilderness,

my soul cried aloud into
my providing rooms,
those empty of hearers,
so that bringing back
the gold,
to purchase the day,
lay within my own silent
voice.
And I looked to the day and
whispered.

Elizabeth

november 9, 2003

winter highwayman

a cold wind came in the night,
blowing, blowing into
midnight's hour
through my south pines,
or so it seemed;
and their voices were like great
fans, in the wind, blowing,
blowing,
weeping above the last insect
chorus,
bringing memory, as itself
a wind,
making sounding fans,
crying in my heart,
my consciousness of time,
of summer passed,
of season and change,

of loss:
and I reached to the spent
runner of autumn,
that I catch
the baton, to press toward
rest on the bed of
winter.

brown leaves, dry and feather-like,
lie below absent moths
which, in their close
recentcy, bejeweled my
lighted chime, whose, its
voice, wept the passing.

A. Noyes/elizabeth

in the night, near midnight (11:45)
November 12, 2003 - coming first,
true cold.

in watchful eye
goldenrod, about, has come
into its finishing, ragweed
if you please;
and sunflowers look with
fatigue to their lord,
he, distancing
into removed, deeper heavens.
leaves, having left their stems,
offer smiles in umbers
and siennas,
almond and chesnut
declaring, however,
gently,
the closing of a season,
a day nearly done.
but, almost like playful sprites,
a juxtaposition in images

comes to pattern,
of radiance,
whose maidenglow, and
sheen which quickens
as starlight, counterpoint
with colors dancing
dust sparkling in lifting—
this lost radiance caresses a
melancholy, beautiful, in
the watchful eye of
memory.

elizabeth

driving / errands
november 13, 2003,
mamma and daddys
anniversary (sixty-two
years)

The Sword

The seasons are the very smiles
of Holy Presence, and
they play my heart
like a mourning lyre;
for in the long travail
to terrestrial provinces,
I left, with my first being,
more than such schedules
allow
so that my yearning is ever,
my homeward angel
filling
my heart to bursting
with the first lily,
reaching up to morning's
anointing;

the leaf drifting, brown
suede, dry and crackled,
following autumn's way;
the rose,
its sweetness in its radiance,
snare in its recalling.
halos and shadow, echo and
winds
seduce my thought, and I
am sentiment bound,
to view in my inward eye
the peace which was,
which waits,
when my fire is ember
into ash, for my fire
does not burn now always,
in fiercest white,
or in the rage of flame,
but burned of
balm remembered, in

distant corners,
inversely warms my need
of constant dwelling,
where conclusions do not arrive
with beauty
such as that of the sword,
true,
of bittersweet.

elizabeth

after book critique
with J. I Good,
november 14, 2003

the mirroring
in fullest Consciousness, my
sudden waking found a
wall
of silence,
that of the fallen hours,
those of birthing morning,
its travail without
voice, but speaking as a
torrent of images
surging about, a very
floodwater
of festival and memory,
into the halls of yesterday.
and I do not wish to journey
there, to wander among
the voices of my
solitude, its quiet bittersweet,
its insistent absences
which with emptynesses,

certain chambers
of my heart.
— to paint out shadows, to allow —
echoes to die; to sound
chimes
with bells, to press old
flesh —
in these would find mortal
my solitude,
but, in these, without a saving
reprieve,
these chambers of absence
would fragment
and fall away,
leaving me, in greatest
truth, less; I must, then,
beside my laughter,
provide a mourning,

that the whole of me leap
forth, full awake to day,
to stay its hours,
having given, left, imaged
in form and fragrance,
the rose,
nourished by its own emptying,
mirroring the fully
bittersweet.

elizabeth

Waiting again,
and remembering,
prompted by a heavy
cloud of dreams in the
night, reminding of
the past, my family,
my sentiments now
6:15, november 23, 2003

a small season

soft adagios held up the
widening silk of dawn,
with rose against purple
lighted behind by a
metaphorical candle,
it to become the full of day,
these hues promising
cold,
and november bowing
to the first chapter of winter
festival, coming
december.
a hawk's cries remind, above
the adagios, a sad
trumpeting to the
assemblage of birds of chill.

my heart, my heart,
rain begins,
soft notes on the dry,
waiting expanse of
brown and gold, but
more,
in my deep inward, it being
somehow good to remember,
and for the all of it,
to weep, inside, companioning
crimson to gold,
whose wet makes again
alive, and near, with
fancied properties which
I can, however in a
small season of moments
hold.

Elizabeth

book review in the
afternoon —
I hope good, well
for J.
November 16, 2003
6:30 – 7:00 AM.
Sunday

as—
(rain coming: to the dry dust of
elizabeth)

—the chimes were beautiful,
for they sounded
every striking of my
heart,
Truly as the words of my
thought, the flesh of
my spirit.
the dark was gentle, holding as the
new purpose of my will, to be
lost in the dark's deep,
as my heart is lost to
such as a first love;
—the wind moved as flowing
water,

as ebonyied, leaping
flame,
as voice to peace of struggle,
as its full joy of content,
a mercy, peace which follows
pain:
yet a night rainbow whose arc
falls into my receiving
heart;
embracing as arms that
hold all the tears
of every night before,
bitter prologue to a new scene,
a painting of sound and
movement,

images in thoughtful
quiet,
sorrow's touch, impotent,

on a bed of hours,
my soul,
within blessing, calling out,
"amen".

elizabeth

2:00 AM, waking
november 18, 2003
rain in advent.
I have been so long, sorrowful,
in the night.

Sabbath's one:
a moment

The day came in on its ancient
assurances, ice-like blue
behind dark riffels,
with paths from the earth
upward of pale coral
and stained ivory;
I heard birdcalls, one, and then
a fancied more, these sounding
in Sabbath stillness.
Written words, just received,
exclaimed with joy, the
musings of my heart
and Holy Presence was in the
echoes of all the systems
of being
my thought could find

the sky painting in by the
magic brush of
coming light,
birdsongs and wheels
turning,
these impetus to their echoes
as hymns of worship.
a peace
visited my fully conscious,
beggar soul,
a filling and nourishing
mystery
a moment of crucifixion,
a lifting of the veil. amen.

elizabeth

just beginning
Chopra's work,
How to know God;
7:00 AM, november 23, 2003

Sabbath's two:
Toward full knowing

I am afraid to Close my eyes;
I fear the arranging of
my thought;
angst shrouds the slowing
of my steps, for in the
between of these
Closings and my next
awareness
sits a Consciousness
most unknown to me,
except in my fear within
an instant's discovery
of its reality;

my steps must become more
deliberate,

my thought and imaging
skirt the casement
of wisdom's larder;
I must drink the sacrament
of giving, build high
my sacrifice of self's
offering,
letting winds take its smoke
turned crimson,
into Holy Presence, gathering
strength
with ableness; to pick up
the glove
of mortality, into victory
of full knowing with
Acceptance.

- a moment, one of many
today, already,
of the portending hound
that is in chase of my
thought;
depersonalization.
7:20 AM, elizabeth
november 23, 2003

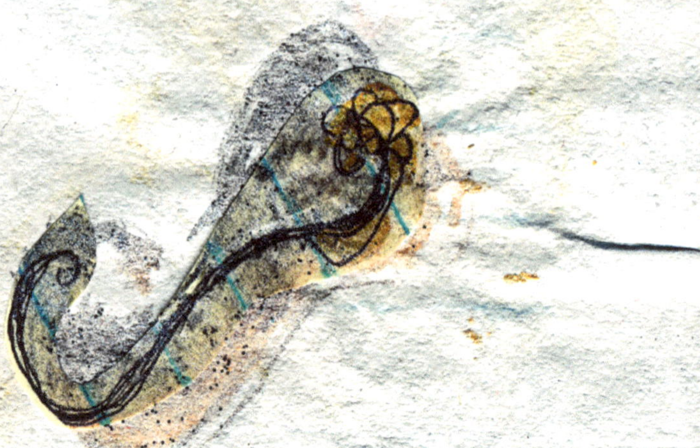

sabbath's three:
early morning sun
like a cell pulsating, the round
of brilliant light broke
through
early morning mists,
and my eye held it
so that I am blinded
as I pen;
for it found me and caught,
as golden as a wedding,
and I could not
free my senses at all,
but waited its instant
of quickly passing, leaving
a bright shape of
glowing dark.

I do not want to hear,
now,
the beating of my heart,
for in its between
spaces lie
the grasp of death, the
sting
of unrelenting, non-
rearranging
eternity,
an unwalked scape in those
moments, yet one familiar
to me

elizabeth

— the sun finding me in
bed,
through the balcony door,
drawing my eyes into it,
holding for only an
intense moment —
so close is the other side.

7:40 AM, November 23, 2003

over and again: The
majesty
of the natural, within
the Cosmos of all Things,
ecstacy
given everyman, in
lelecon
of giving and receiving.

— note to verse immediately
behind, as the sun moved
across the sky, westward!
8:10 AM, november 23, 2003
Elizabeth

note: Sabbath's three, review

I do not wish to write
more, for I am
fatigued
with emoting, of
looking at my sentiments
those known, and those
only surmised.

Elizabeth

sabbath's four:
storms of soul

silently hang the hours,
still, forgotten leaves in
soft autumn winds;
an ambiance of storm
dresses
my rooms, in looking out,
but inside the chambers of my
heart,
battle holds with unhappy
movement
against a constant, unfulfilled
yearning.
your voice has been absent
to me,

As those of my fellows
and kin,
These among trifles of
mislaid words
and presuming spirits;
almost irony, the ease with
which the white of trust
could hang among
the hours,
the leaves, the chambers
of my heart—
how much so, but nein, for
some storms are of soul
and do not easily
or quickly, if
harshly, pass, as in
woodlands, meadows, the abundant
sky.

1:00 pm, november 23, 2003,
resuming the poet stance,
alone with the
wall clock,
fearing all manner of
storms.
elizabeth

Sabbath's five:
evening prayer

forgive and strengthen;
hold me in safety and
love.
let flowers of trust and
beauty
Grow out the musings of
my heart.
let me be gentle, let me find
wisdom,
The path, the steps to quiet
peace.

elizabeth

november 23, 2003
eventide

elizabeth
-november 29, 2003

into my deep
down into the deep is where
I feel, beyond virtue,
or malice,
but into fear of being
left when all the
girls
are asked to dance.
to the side, going down, lie
pain and loss, as
with summer into its
passing,
shortened peace, good
Coming to great fatigue,
These weighted against joyful
knowings and sentiments
sweet enough to image,
in reflection,
purple leaning into rose

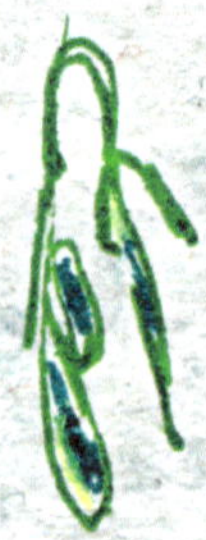

in the sky's winter
Cold.
in my deep I am, truly,
infant with soul, loving
and hurting
as the day steps forth,
unfolding,
holding that which I
can in a desperate
clinging to the hand
that takes mine.
In my deep, I can eat and
drink the passions of
my soul, its
wideness, its smallness,
but
like a lover found out,
I find that I stand

naked,
no cloth being to cover
me, and I then feel,
the pain of the greatest
deep,
past the dance,
that of losing to the infidelity
to caring beyond my deep,
more than the insistent
scrutiny of my own
self, to find
pleasant indulgences
but beside the resulting
certainty of first
beauty in giving to
another,
his bounty finding

its way back to me,

oh love, I did not search
you out, but with idle
prattle,
left you alone; please
forgive me, tonight
I hear, still, your unhappy
soundings, words,
hesitations, silences,
this night of sabbath,
of your return.

elizabeth

sunday night, 9:30 pm.
november 31, 2003

– waiting, concluded,
beginning again.

Epistle Claire

Elizabeth has enjoyed writing almost all of her life, but she did not enter the genre of poetry until she became ill in 1965, and it was not until the early seventies, with her second marriage, and some improvement in emotional health, that she took up her pen with an inspired discipline. Some good beginning work was done, but it was laid aside shortly because of her continuing illness and unhappy relationship with her husband. No additional work was done until the mid-nineties, when, following her husband's death and convalescing from an automobile accident, to eventually retire from teaching that she began again. Since then, she has written almost every day and often in deepest night. Her work is uneven, but much of it is the work of a passionate imagist exploring the weightier matters of life alongside those lighter – and always the beautiful, her said "antidote" to despair.

Elizabeth's work is spontaneous, and inclusive of all that evokes her thought; it is handwritten and dressed and reworked very seldom, the form of free verse providing this advantage. Nature is the canvas on which her pen draws the pictures her mind conceives – and many of her pieces are worthy in wisdom and loveliness, the undercurrent of darkness from her bipolar illness always shadowing the light that has continued an insistent presence. She lives alone in her country home near Jackson, Mississippi under the care of Dr. John Norton of The University of Mississippi Medical Center. She amuses herself with a variety of creative past-times – painting, sculpting, music, reading, sewing (hand stitching), flowers (drying and pressing into designs), and of late, fencing. She enjoys entertaining the company of a very plethora of friends and their activities together. Her autobiography, <u>I Elizabeth</u> was published in late summer, 2007 by Trafford.

The hickory tree from "Songs. . ." is one that stands before Elizabeth's home, affectionately referred to as "Fallen Timbers" by her late husband, Richard. It appears in autumn dress, as she remembered and painted it, in spring 2008.

April 3, 2008

Hickory in Autumn, Two

In its own time, again, the hickory stands,
Bountiful in beautygold,
Just as it always has;
And I stand in its presence,
With humbled awe,
As I always do,
That in this metaphorical Devine
Face of nature,
There is remembrance continuing,
So, as it always has,
Offering absolute, golden
Joy and hope.

Elizabeth

November, 2007

www.ingramcontent.com/pod-product-compliance
Ingram Content Group UK Ltd.
Pitfield, Milton Keynes, MK11 3LW, UK
UKHW061023310726
14090UKWH00023B/13
* 9 7 8 1 4 2 5 1 8 4 7 9 7 *